Canvas Of The Mind

Tela Simao

BookLeaf Publishing
India | USA | UK

Tela Simao

Presentation by *BookLeaf Publishing*

Web: www.bookleafpub.com

E-mail: info@bookleafpub.com

ISBN: 978-93-5744-467-5

First edition 2022

BALANCE

What's the difference between an angel or a demon?
Serve the same purpose, both a product of God's semen
Brightest lights cast the darkest shadows
One without the other is like the thorns without the rose
Experience ugliness to appreciate the beauty
Sometimes like the face that tags along with the booty
Tired of living life on patience is a virtue
Deal with past traumas before they come back to curse you
Ain't got no time for shepherding lost souls
Many stay stuck causing traffic at cross roads
Find your balance when you let go of the dead load.

A NEW DAWN

I look up, I see judgement in the mind and hatred in the heart. I know not if I am the child of God or the Devil's angel, a paradox of resolve. Yearning for light, neighbouring darkness; my life, an oxymoron. Bliss in the abyss burdened by trepidation. Accept my light or neglect my darkness. Red or blue, I choose purple for I, too, am a creation of God. Inhabitant of a mirror maze of eyes proclaiming a misconceived perception of my nature, the very balance of life.

LENSE

Living to die yet dying to live, same statement, different spectrum, infinite lenses. A feared truth, cryptonite to illusions. What shall pass shall never fall, what shall fall may never pass. Break the shackles, indulge in the limitless. Find what was once lost, a new direction to no destination, a journey with no comprehension only acceptance. Cruising forward but looking back. Limping back set on looking forward. In pursuit of direction, the first step is to make a move, only then will one start to grasp the illusion on the concept of direction. Walking straight but somehow stuck in a loop, taking turns for adventure to pierce a hole in the unbreakable, incomprehensible cycle.

WHY NOT?

Walk on the brink of sanity making love to death
Life a sin, a curse for the blessed
Shackled minds for the limitless within
The hopeful pray as a believer I answer.

LOST

Minds are stolen goods like products
Bought and sold for profit
Brain functions intertwined with toxic
Nobody sitting at the table of house deposits
Beating hearts victims to hypnosis
Learn the value of self, not of notice
In time, cross a Red Sea like Moses.

DARK LIGHT

In absence of light, darkness provides
Running deep, the roots of an unyielding tree
The warrior within bruised from the lack of belief
Trust in essence, pivotal to survival
Starts with self and ends with being
Cataclysmic thoughts, a reboot for the mind
Checkpoint saved; a new beginning.

IT IS WHAT IT IS

Labelling things we don’t understand as mental
health
Scared to confront past demons, call it
depression
Fearful of future fallen angels, call it anxiety
Living with both call it the present.

THE SHEPHERD’S CALLING

Without a villain no need for a hero
Talk money, a gathering, the shepherd’s calling
Brothers falling to greed, a mother’s mourning
No loyalty in creed better watch your hero

RAINDROPS

Rain pours
Then it stops
Summer comes
Then it's hot
Everyday
A body drops
Drop drop
Nonstop

How long
For it to stop?
Live fast
Die young
A mother at home praying for her son
God damn
Another soul
Grim Reaper's on a roll
No hesitation
Just snatched his soul
Another body
Just had to go
On a t-shirt for a month or so
Then back to business
You know how it goes.

UNVEIL

The original victim to the casualties of existence
Layered by pain and traumas, an innocent core
Mellow aura concealed, weakness,
misconceived strength
Broken, the aftermath of the beautiful burden
Construction of physical and spiritual resilience
Healing in own design of comfort pursued by
others, power
Upset the balance and the natural nurturing
habitat converts to chaotic destruction
An implosion of suppressed sentiments
Misplaced love exhibited in anguish
A force to be reckoned
A being to be understood.

LOST X FOUND

Be a found voyager not a lost wonderer
The void you seek to fill seeks to replenish you too
Grass is greener where you water it
Dig out the weeds, start a new
Let the soil invest in your roots.

BACK & FORTH

My eyes, your mirror
My scent, your perfume
My patience, your virtue
My touch, your revelation.

NATURE

Passion, walking the streets of moonlit cities. Vandalised curls, graffitied bodies capitulating to the call of the night, succumbing to the twilight nature.

A cool breeze scrambles the warmth of the birds and the bees in the air, a spine shivering sensation. Butterfly feelings with stern faces, a spectacle in essence.

A loud silence breaks the room. Therapeutic raindrops hit the windowsill, dancing to the rhythm of pacing hearts.

SEIGE

Infatuating whispers magnetised with seduction. Hidden sensitivities, soaked to the stroke. Once a core, now just a mirage. Senses built to withstand a siege, unfamiliar with the tenderness of relief.

LOVE

I love you not for how you love me
But how you love yourself
It reflects onto me.

CIRCLE OR TRINITY

Summer nights, winter mornings
Spring to life, autumn callings
Life and death, the simplicity
Expectations the complications of beliefs
Keeping up with reality, losing touch with self
False sense of accomplishment
Conditioned to inhabit faithless pretences
Mind, body, soul foreign tongues, contrasting
ideologies.

TARRAXO DO GUETTO

Movements of art, innovations of imagination,
embodiment of action. Escapade on the dance
floor. A convoluting tale of body and mind.
A phenomenon within.
Minds sync, souls trust, and senses sparkle.
Imprisoned aggression, absolved fervour.

ELYSIAN FIELDS

Waterfalls in the presence of the honey glazed nectar, landslides in the hear of the thunder. Marvelling at the bespoke splendour of the unscathed Elysian Fields, gods walk amongst gods.

THE PARCHED

Longing for touch, lusting for warmth. Fiends of despair, monstrosities, a plague to the surface lurking the outskirts of paradise conspiring for a soul of ecstasy to quench their thirst.

THE CONVO

I sent you my heaven
You replied with your hell.

LEGACY

No anger shall burden my heart
No fear shall bitter my mind
No despair shall conquer my lungs
I let the pain course through my veins but it shall not mix with my blood.

www.ingramcontent.com/pod-product-compliance
Lightning Source LLC
Chambersburg PA
CBHW062111140826
49812CB00058B/1305
9789357444675